CHALLENGING SCIENCE AND LITERACY ACTIVITIES FOR K–9 STUDENTS: THE CRICKET CHRONICLES

Student Edition

Catherine E. Matthews

My Cricket Chronicles Learning Log

Rowman & Littlefield Education
Lanham, Maryland • Toronto • Oxford
2006

Published in the United States of America
by Rowman & Littlefield Education
A Division of Rowman & Littlefield Publishers, Inc.
A wholly owned subsidary of The Rowman & Littlefield Publishing Group, Inc.
4501 Forbes Boulevard, Suite 200, Lanham, Maryland 20706
www.rowmaneducation.com

PO Box 317
Oxford
OX2 9RU, UK

Student Edition   ISBN-10: 1-57886-358-9 / ISBN-13: 978-1-57886-358-7
Teacher Edition   ISBN-10: 1-57886-496-8 / ISBN-13: 978-1-57886-496-6

∞™ The paper used in this publication meets the minimum requirements of American National Standard for
Information Sciences—Permanence of Paper for Printed Library Materials, ANSI/NISO Z39.48-1992.
Manufactured in the United States of America.

CONTENTS

WELCOME TO *THE CRICKET CHRONICLES*

Dear Student,

Welcome to *The Cricket Chronicles*. Over the next several weeks, you will be learning about crickets in your classroom. You will be reading about crickets and writing about crickets. You will be doing activities to find out about what crickets like and what they don't like. You will record your information in this *Learning Log* called *My Cricket Chronicles Learning Log*. You will be able to share your *Learning Log* with your family. When you complete your cricket studies, you will know more about crickets than anyone you know and you can teach other people about crickets. Have fun!

Love,

The Cricket Chronicler

STUDENT QUESTIONNAIRE

Complete this questionnaire before beginning activity #1.

What do you know about crickets already? Think about what you already know about crickets.

What do crickets look like?

_____

_____

_____

What kinds of sounds do crickets make?

_____

_____

_____

Where do crickets live?

_____

_____

_____

In the space below, write one or more things that you already know about crickets. On the next page, draw a big picture of a cricket. Try to make your cricket ten times larger than a real cricket. This is called 10X.

_____

_____

_____

Draw a large picture of a cricket. Try to make your picture ten times (10X) bigger than a real cricket.

ORGANIZATION OF *MY CRICKET CHRONICLES* LEARNING LOG

My *Cricket Chronicles Learning Log* contains 31 different activities. Each activity has one or more essential questions that you should be able to answer when you have completed the activity. You can use any blank space in your *Learning Log* to answer the essential question or questions for each activity.

Each of the 31 activities has three parts: the Essential Question(s), and sections called "What do I need?" and "What do I do?" These sections tell you about any materials or supplies that you will need and they also tell you how to go about doing the activity. Your teacher may give you additional information, too.

You will complete some of these activities by yourself. Other activities will be completed by a small group of students. Your teacher will tell you whether you will work alone or with other classmates on each activity. Your teacher might not ask you to do every activity in this *Learning Log* but after you finish the project in school, you will be able to keep your log and complete any activities you did not get to do in school at home with your parent's/guardian's permission.

Photos courtesy of University of North Carolina Greensboro Creative Services.

FINDING CRICKETS & DESCRIBING CRICKET HABITATS

ESSENTIAL QUESTIONS

- What do crickets look like?
- Where do crickets live?
- Where do we find crickets in their natural habitats?
- How can I use what I observe to describe where crickets live?
- How can I make pictures in my mind to describe cricket habitats after reading information about crickets?

WHAT DO I NEED?

- Crayons
- Map of schoolyard

WHAT DO I DO?

Your teacher will give you a map of your schoolyard.

1. Take your map outside and mark places where you find crickets on your map. Do not pick up crickets today.
2. After you come back inside, complete the activities and answer the questions on the next page.

Write three or four sentences about the places (habitats) where you found crickets.

_____

_____

_____

_____

Draw a picture of one place where you found crickets.

Think about where you found crickets. If you were a cricket, what would make these good places to live? List as many describing words (adjectives) as you can.

_____

_____

_____

_____

_____

_____

RESPECTING CRICKETS

(2)

 **ESSENTIAL QUESTION**

How can I keep my crickets healthy and happy while I am studying their behaviors?

 **WHAT DO I NEED?**

- Pencil

WHAT DO I DO?

Listen carefully as your teacher reads the instructions. Then, read each of the sentences below and decide if you agree or disagree with each one. Circle "Agree" if you think that the statement is true. Circle "Disagree" if you think it is not true or not completely true. Next, complete the ethics pledge.

1. Crickets are living animals.	Agree / Disagree
2. Crickets need food, water, and a place to live.	Agree / Disagree
3. Crickets can feel pain when you squeeze them hard or injure their body parts.	Agree / Disagree
4. It is okay to injure a cricket for fun because it is just an insect.	Agree / Disagree
5. In order to be allowed to study living animals in class, I should try to handle them carefully.	Agree / Disagree
6. Crickets are important creatures in nature. We need crickets.	Agree / Disagree

Ethics Pledge

for

The Cricket Chronicles

I, _____ , do hereby promise to

(your name)

handle all crickets carefully. I also promise to do my best to provide for my crickets'

basic needs: air, soil, water, and food during *The Cricket Chronicles*.

_____

(signed)

COUNTING CRICKETS THAT LIVE IN YOUR SCHOOLYARD

ESSENTIAL QUESTIONS

How can we determine the size of the cricket population in our schoolyard?
How can we measure the length of a cricket?

WHAT DO I NEED?

- Insect net
- Tweezers or forceps
- One small bottle (0.7 oz.) of correction fluid
- Ruler

WHAT DO I DO?

Each person in your group will have one job. Everyone will get to do each job twice.

The *cricket catcher* uses the insect net to catch as many crickets as possible in a certain number of minutes. Your teacher will tell you how many minutes to spend catching crickets.

The *cricket holder* manages the crickets caught so that they can be marked, holds each cricket for the marker, and measures the length of each cricket with a flexible ruler or a string marked with measurements.

The *cricket marker* places one small white dot on the thorax (the middle segment of the cricket) of each cricket caught.

The *data recorder* writes down the information on the table on the next page.

Table 3.1. Crickets Counted, Measured, & Marked

Name of Cricket Catcher	Number of Crickets Caught	Length of Crickets Caught	Number of Crickets Marked
1.			
2.			
3.			
4.			
1.			
2.			
3.			
4.			

Glen and Clayton collecting crickets with sweep nets

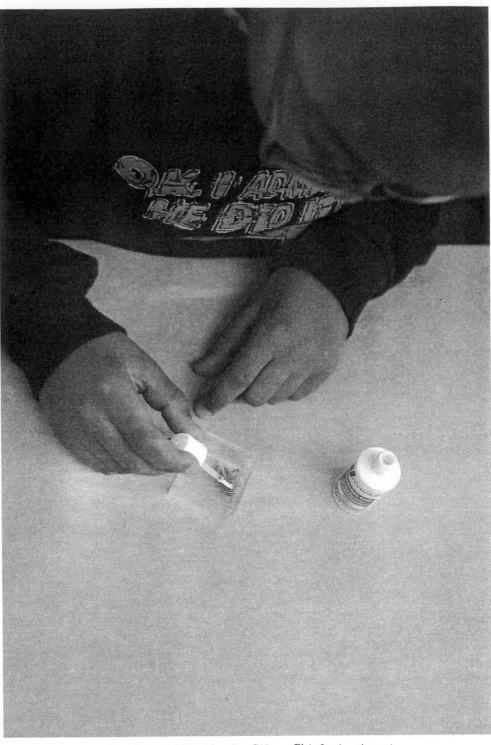

Glen marks a cricket with a dot of Wite-out™ before he releases it

COUNTING CRICKETS AGAIN & COLLECTING CRICKETS

ESSENTIAL QUESTION

How can we estimate how many crickets live on our school grounds?

WHAT DO I NEED?

- Insect net
- Tweezers or forceps
- Ruler

WHAT DO I DO?

You are going to count crickets again. The jobs are almost the same as those that you had for the first cricket counting activity.

The *cricket catcher* uses the insect net to catch as many crickets as possible in a certain number of minutes. Your teacher will tell you how many minutes to spend catching crickets.

The *cricket holder* measures the length of each cricket with a flexible ruler or string marked with measurements.

The *data recorder* writes down the length of each cricket on the following table.

The *calculator* will compute totals and share them.

Table 4.1.   Crickets Counted, Measured, & Marked Again

Name of Cricket Catcher	Number of Crickets Caught	Length of Crickets Caught	Number of Marked Crickets Caught
1.			
2.			
3.			
4.			
1.			
2.			
3.			
4.			

Look at the information (data) on table 3.1 and compare it with the data on this table.

Were all of the crickets that you caught today already marked?   Yes / No   (Circle the correct response)

How many were marked? _____ How many were unmarked? _____

Your teacher will help you calculate the estimated number of crickets in the schoolyard: _____

5

DESIGNING & CREATING CRICKET HABITATS

 ESSENTIAL QUESTION

What kinds of habitats do crickets prefer?

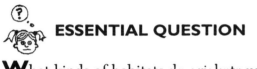 **WHAT DO I NEED?**

- Crayons
- Pencils
- Crickets
- Glue stick
- Items that can be used to make cricket homes (containers, soil, cotton balls for water, and bottle lids to hold wet cotton balls)
- Camera

 **WHAT DO I DO?**

Think about where you found your crickets. Then, follow the instructions on the next page.

MY CRICKET'S HOME

Draw a picture of the cricket home that you would like to make below. When you are finished, show your teacher your drawing. Look at your list of words that describe cricket habitats from Activity #1. This should help you think about what you will need to make your cricket a comfortable home.

1. Make your cricket home and then move your crickets to their new home.
2. Draw a picture of your cricket home or take a picture with a digital camera and then you can paste the picture below.

6

READING ABOUT CRICKETS

ESSENTIAL QUESTIONS

What can we learn about crickets from reading books and book selections about crickets?

How can we use what we already know about crickets to help us understand and learn more from books about crickets?

WHAT DO I NEED?

- A book or pages from a book about crickets
- Pencil

WHAT DO I DO?

Write the title of your book below. Then, write your answers in the table on the next page.

Title of book: _____

Table 6.1. Reading About Crickets

K—What do we already KNOW about crickets?	W—What do we WANT to learn about crickets in the book that we will read?	L— What did we LEARN about crickets from reading the book?	S—What do we STILL want to learn about crickets?

Reading books about crickets

Glen works on his KWL chart about crickets

COMPARING KIDS AND CRICKETS

ESSENTIAL QUESTION

How are kids and crickets alike and how are they different?

WHAT DO I NEED?

- Cricket in insect box or hand lens
- Pencil

WHAT DO I DO?

1. Draw a picture of yourself and label your body parts. Be sure to draw your legs, feet, arms, hands, head, eyes, nose, ears, and lungs.
2. Look at your cricket. Draw a picture of your cricket. Label all of the body parts that you already know.
3. Now, complete the Venn Diagram comparing yourself and your cricket.

 This is me.

 This is my cricket.

Complete the following Venn diagram to compare you and your cricket.

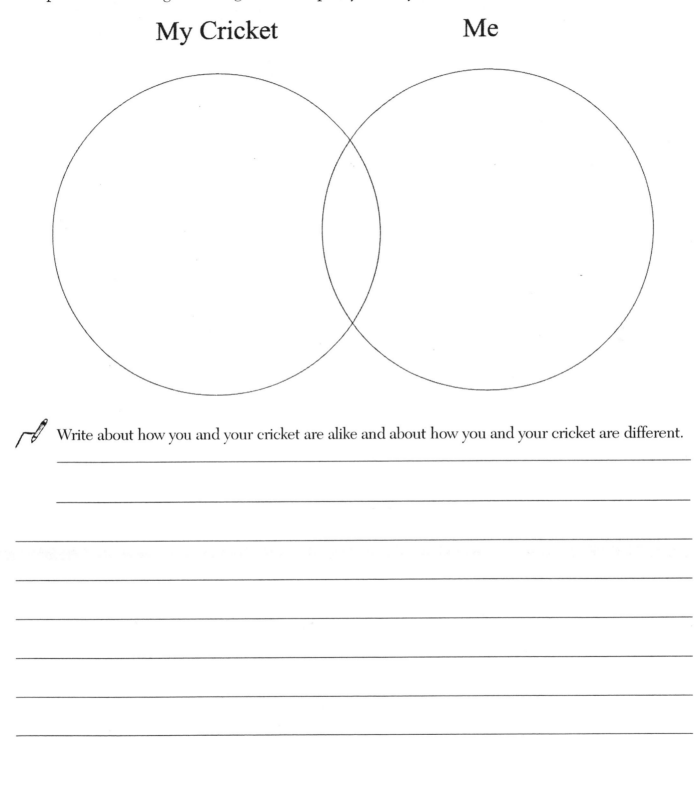

Write about how you and your cricket are alike and about how you and your cricket are different.

_____

_____

_____

_____

_____

_____

_____

Completing a Venn diagram comparing crickets and kids

8

LOOKING AT CRICKETS

ESSENTIAL QUESTIONS

What makes a cricket a cricket?
What makes a cricket an insect?
What makes a cricket an arthropod?
Where are cricket body parts and how do these body parts help the cricket survive?

WHAT DO I NEED?

- Crickets
- Pencils
- Hand lenses
- Insect boxes
- Small drinking cups

WHAT DO I DO?

1. Look closely at your cricket with a hand lens. If it is hard for you to see the body parts of crickets, use the big picture on the next page to help you find all of the parts of your cricket.
2. Work with your group to answer the questions on the following pages.

Anatomy of the Cricket

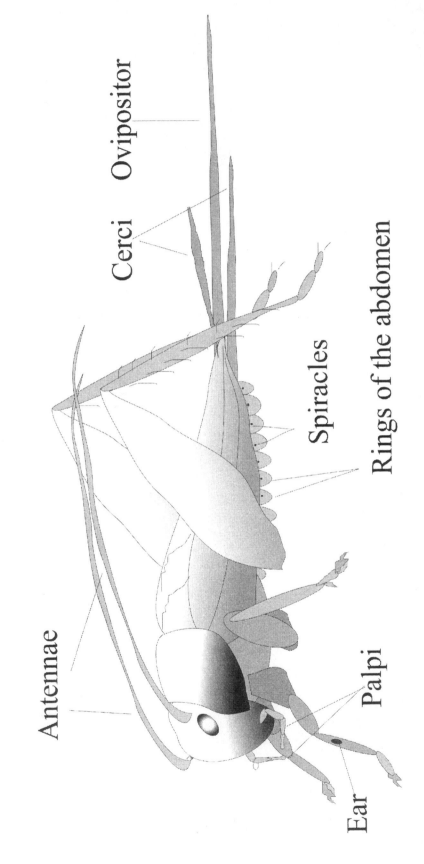

Ovipositor

Cerci

Rings of the abdomen

Spiracles

Antennae

Palpi

Ear

CRICKET BODY PARTS

1. How many eyes do you see? _____

2. How many ears do you see? Are a cricket's ears on its head? _____

3. Where are their ears and why are they there? _____

4. Why do crickets need to hear? _____

   _____

5. How many legs do crickets have? _____

6. How many legs are on each side of the cricket's body? _____

7. Does your cricket have antennae? Trace the antennae on the cricket diagram. _____

8. Why do you think that the antennae are so long? _____

   _____

9. What do you think the antennae are used for? _____

   _____

10. How many wings does your cricket have? What body part are the wings attached to? _____

   _____

11. How do you think your cricket breathes? _____

   _____

Olivia observing crickets in a cricket home and Austin looking at a cricket in an insect observation box

CONSTRUCTING MODELS OF CRICKETS

ESSENTIAL QUESTION

What can I learn about crickets from constructing a model cricket?

WHAT DO I NEED?

- A paper model of a cricket
- Construction paper
- Pencil
- Scissors
- Glue stick

WHAT DO I DO?

There are three different models of crickets in this *Learning Log*. There is a mole cricket, a tree cricket, and a field cricket. Choose the type of cricket model that you would like to make.

1. First, label the following cricket body parts on the back of the parts of the model: leg, wing, abdomen, head, eye and ear.
2. Then, cut out your model and glue the parts together to make a model.
3. Compare and contrast the three different models of crickets.

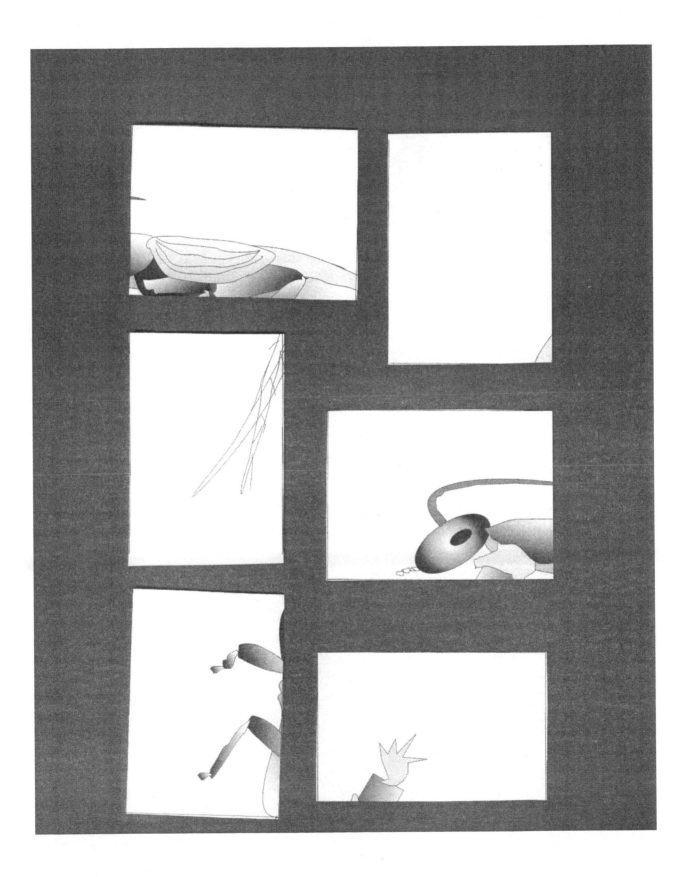

10

READING MORE ABOUT CRICKETS &
USING CRICKET WORDS

ESSENTIAL QUESTION

What vocabulary words can we learn from reading that will help us understand more about crickets?

WHAT DO I NEED?

- Pencil
- "Facts about Crickets" Information Sheet

WHAT DO I DO?

1. After your teacher tells you to begin, write one long sentence using all of the words below.
2. Or, write six different sentences using one of the words in one box in each sentence.
3. Have one person in your group write the sentence(s), while the other people in the group tell the recorder what to write.
4. After you finish, follow along as your teacher reads aloud "Facts about Crickets."

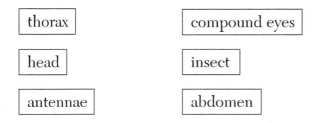

thorax	compound eyes
head	insect
antennae	abdomen

FACTS ABOUT CRICKETS

There are many interesting facts about crickets and other insects. Let's read some of these facts.

Crickets have three pairs of legs and three body parts. Because crickets have six legs and three body parts, they are *insects*. Insects are small animals and usually have wings. Crickets and other insects do not have bones on the inside. Their skeleton is on the outside.

Female or girl crickets have long tubes that stick out from their *abdomens*, or back parts of their bodies. Eggs travel through this tube. Crickets lay these eggs in small, tight places.

When they are first hatched, crickets do not have any wings on their thorax, which is the middle part of an insect's body. Crickets breathe through holes on the sides of the *thorax* and abdomen.

Crickets have body parts that help them find out about the world around them. On the cricket's *head*, which is the front part of an insect's body, are the *antennae*. Antennae are feelers that help crickets find out about what is around them. Crickets have five eyes, but you can only see the big *compound eyes* on the top of a cricket's head. These compound eyes are the cricket's largest eyes. These eyes are on both sides of the cricket's head. Compound eyes are eyes that look like one eye, but they are really many smaller eyes that are close together.

Now, read the "Facts about Crickets" on your own. Write sentences that tell the meaning of the words that were written in *italics* in the story. You may write one long sentence, or you may write one sentence with each word. Have one person in the group write the sentence, while the other people in the group tell the recorder what to write.

Ms. Vass using a Good Readers Chart with her students

COLORING CRICKET BODY PARTS

ESSENTIAL QUESTION

How can coloring cricket body parts help me learn and remember more of these parts?

WHAT DO I NEED?

- Cricket diagrams
- Crayons

WHAT DO I DO?

The picture at the top of the next page is a male (boy) cricket.

The picture at the bottom of the page is a female (girl) cricket.

Scientists use the symbol ♂ for boys.
Scientists use the symbol ♀ for girls.

These same symbols are used for male and female animals of all kinds, including crickets and kids.

Color the following body parts with these colors:

Legs = Green   Antennae = Brown   Wings = Black
Spiracles = Purple Eye = Orange   Ear = White
Cerci = Green   Palpi = Red   Ovipositor = Blue

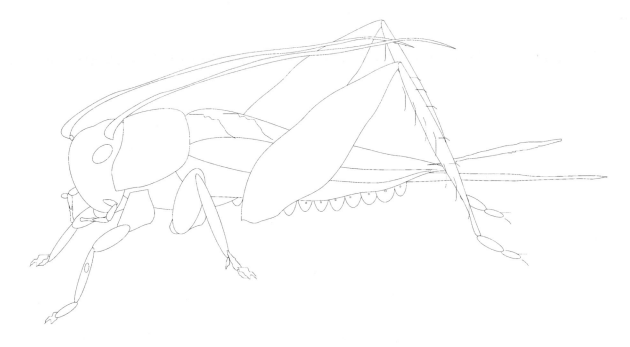

Color the three parts of the cricket's body with these colors:

Head = Yellow

Thorax (or middle part where wings and legs attach) = Green

Abdomen (back part) = Blue

(12)

IDENTIFYING CRICKET STORY PARTS

ESSENTIAL QUESTION

How can knowing about the parts of a story help me better understand books about crickets?

WHAT DO I NEED?

- Pencil

WHAT DO I DO?

You have been learning about the parts of stories.

1. Listen to the story that your teacher reads aloud.
2. As your teacher reads a story about crickets, write down the parts of the story in the table on the next page.

Table 12.1. Parts of Stories

Part of Story	Details about this specific story
Title of Book	
Setting	
Main Events	
Problem	
Solution	
Ending	

Now that you have listened to a story about crickets, write your own cricket story. Remember to use all the story parts that you have been learning about. You may use the bottom of the page to illustrate your story.

_____

_____

_____

_____

_____

_____

_____

⓭

FINDING CRICKET HABITAT PREFERENCES

 **ESSENTIAL QUESTIONS**

Where do crickets live?
What kinds of habitats do crickets prefer?

 WHAT DO I NEED?

- Clear container
- Dry sand
- Wet sand
- Soil
- Leaves and grass mixture
- Eight crickets from your habitat
- Pencil

 **WHAT DO I DO?**

Answer the question below and then complete the group activity on the next page.

Which habitat do you think your cricket will like better?

1. Wet or Dry? Why? _____

_____

2. Soil or Leaves & Grass? Why? _____

_____

Get together with your group and do the following things:

Day One

1. Put dry sand in one corner of your container.
2. Put wet sand in another corner of your container.
3. Put soil in the third corner.
4. Put the leaves and grass into the last corner.
5. Then put eight crickets from your habitat into this new container.

Day Two

Record where you find crickets at the times indicated in table 13.1.

Day Three

The next day, answer the last four questions about your experiment.

CRICKET HABITAT PREFERENCES RECORDING SHEET

Write the number of crickets closest to each corner at each of the times given.

Table 13.1.   Cricket Habitat Preferences

	Dry Sand	Wet Sand	Soil	Leaves & Grass
9 AM				
11AM				
1 PM				
3 PM				
Total				

Questions on the Habitat Experiment

1. Where did you find most of your crickets?

    _____

    _____

    _____

    _____

2. Why do you think your crickets liked that area best?

    _____

    _____

    _____

    _____

3. Did your crickets move from one place to another?

    _____

    _____

    _____

    _____

4. Did your crickets stay where you thought they would? Why did you choose this area?

    _____

    _____

    _____

    _____

Investigating crickets' preferences for different substrates

CRICKET CONNOISSEURS

ESSENTIAL QUESTION

What foods do crickets eat in their natural habitats, and what animals eat crickets?

WHAT DO I NEED?

- Pictures of the animals and plants listed here: leaf, grass blade, mouse, bird, frog, ant, turtle, spider, plant, mushroom, tomato, and lizard
- Scissors
- Glue stick

WHAT DO I DO?

It is hard to study crickets outside because they are so small and because they like to live under objects. Nevertheless, scientists have studied crickets and found out about the foods that crickets eat. They also know about other animals that eat crickets. Both things that eat crickets and things that crickets eat are pictured. Cut out the pictures and paste them in the circles on the next page. The arrows point to the animals that are eating the cricket; these animals are called *predators*. Another set of arrows points from other animals and plants to the cricket, indicating that these items are being eaten by the cricket. These items are called *prey items*.

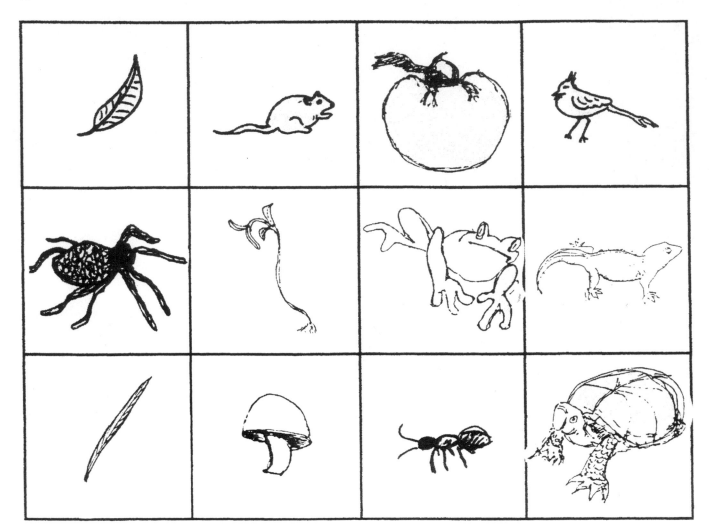

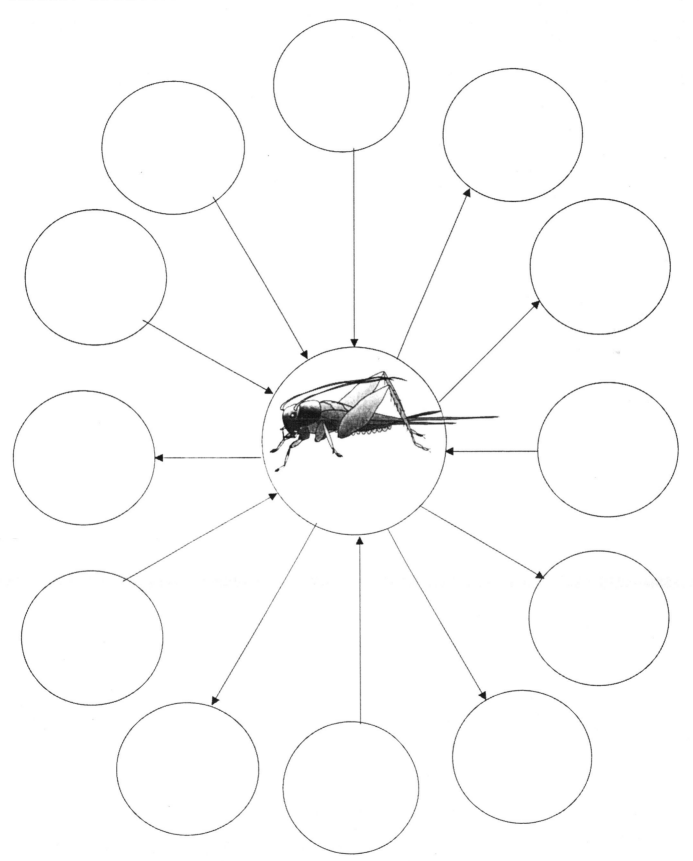

15

THINKING ABOUT FEEDING CRICKETS
& FEEDING CRICKETS

 ## ESSENTIAL QUESTIONS

Can I design and conduct an investigation that allows me to test two foods to see which food crickets prefer to eat in captivity?

What foods do crickets in captivity prefer?

 ## WHAT DO I NEED?

- Pencil
- Clear empty containers
- Different kinds of cricket food
- 2 to 4 crickets for each student group

 ## WHAT DO I DO?

Work with your group to answer the following questions on the table on the next page.

Table 15.1.   Thinking about Feeding Cricket

Questions	Answers
What foods do you think crickets like to eat?	
Why do you think they like those foods?	
What foods would you like to see if your crickets would eat?	
If you were a cricket, what foods would you eat?	

Make up an experiment like the one that follows to test which foods your crickets like best. Write or draw about your experimental plans on the next page. Show your test plan to your teacher. Your teacher will tell you what to do next.

A SAMPLE CRICKET FOOD PREFERENCES EXPERIMENT

1. Ask a question. For example, "What foods do crickets like to eat?"
2. Make a prediction. For example, "I think crickets like to eat carrots."
3. Make up an experiment to see if your prediction is right. For example, "I will put a cricket in a box with carrots and then see if any bits of carrot are missing after a day."
4. Do the experiment and record your observations. For example, "I observed that pieces of the carrot were missing the next day."
5. Decide if your prediction was true or false. For example, "My prediction was true because the crickets ate the carrots."
6. Write an answer to your question based on your experiment. For example, "I found that crickets eat carrots."

MY PROPOSED CRICKET EXPERIMENT

1. My question.

_____

_____

_____

_____

2. My prediction.

_____

_____

_____

_____

3. My proposed experiment to see if my prediction is right.

_____

_____

_____

_____

_____

_____

_____

Get your teacher's approval before conducting your experiment. Your teacher can initial here when he or she has approved your experiment._____
Now, conduct your experiment and answer the following questions.

4. Do the experiment and record your observations.

_____

_____

_____

_____

_____

_____

_____

5. Was your prediction was true or false? _____

6. Write an answer to your question based on your experiment.

_____

_____

_____

16

LIFESTYLES OF CRICKETS

ESSENTIAL QUESTION

Do crickets prefer a solitary or a social existence?

WHAT DO I NEED?

Per group:
- 1 container
- 6 paper baking cups (all one color)
- 6 crickets
- Scissors
- Pencil

WHAT DO I DO?

Answer the four questions below and then complete the activity on the next page.

1. Do you think that crickets like to live together? Why?

2. Do you think that more than one cricket lives in one home? Why?

3. Do you think that all crickets have their own homes? Why?

4. When you find crickets outside, do you find them in groups or alone? Why?

ACTIVITY

1. Cut a door for your cricket into the side of each paper baking cup. Place these cups in your new habitat. Space them out enough so that the crickets can walk in between them. Place six of your crickets into this new habitat.
2. Wait for two days before you make your observations.
3. Complete the table below. Tell what you observed. Write about whether you think crickets in their natural habitats live together or live alone.

Table 16.1. Cricket Lifestyles

How many crickets were under each baking cup?

Observation Time	Cup 1	Cup 2	Cup 3	Cup 4	Cup 5	Cup 6
9 AM						
11 AM						
1 PM						

17

MEASURING AND COMPARING LEG LENGTHS

 ## ESSENTIAL QUESTIONS

How does my leg length compare to a cricket's leg length?
How does my leg length compare to my height?
How does a cricket's leg length compare to its body length?

 ## WHAT DO I NEED?

- One dead cricket or cricket molt
- Yardstick or ruler
- Pencil
- A 12-inch length of string
- Marker

 ## WHAT DO I DO?

Working with a partner, carefully measure the length of each leg of your dead cricket or cricket molt.

1. Measure only the legs on one side of the cricket's body. Begin measuring by finding where the leg meets the body (on the thorax). Using string, trace the length of the leg. Fold the string along the bends in the leg and then mark the total length on the string with a marker.
2. Measure your string using the ruler.
3. Write your answers on the next page.

Using your table of measurements, complete the following chart:

Cricket Measurements

Front Leg: _____

Middle Leg: _____

Back Leg: _____

*Body Length: _____

Measure the length of the body of the cricket from its mouth to the end of its abdomen.
  (*Note: If you have a girl cricket, be sure to stop at the abdomen. Do not include the length of the ovipositor.)

Circle the longest measurement.

Now answer these questions.

  1. Which leg is longest? _____

  2. How much longer than the next longest leg? _____

  3. Why do you think that the longest leg is so long? _____

     _____

     _____

Body Length of Cricket: _____

My Measurements

Leg: _____

Height: _____

Circle the longest measurement.

Now measure your body parts listed below.

Your body length from head to feet: _____

Your leg length from waist to heel: _____

Compare your body length and your leg length to your cricket's body length and leg length.

Make two bar graphs, one that shows cricket leg length and cricket body length and the other that shows your leg length and your body length.

Write about how they are the same or how they are different.

_____

_____

_____

_____

_____

_____

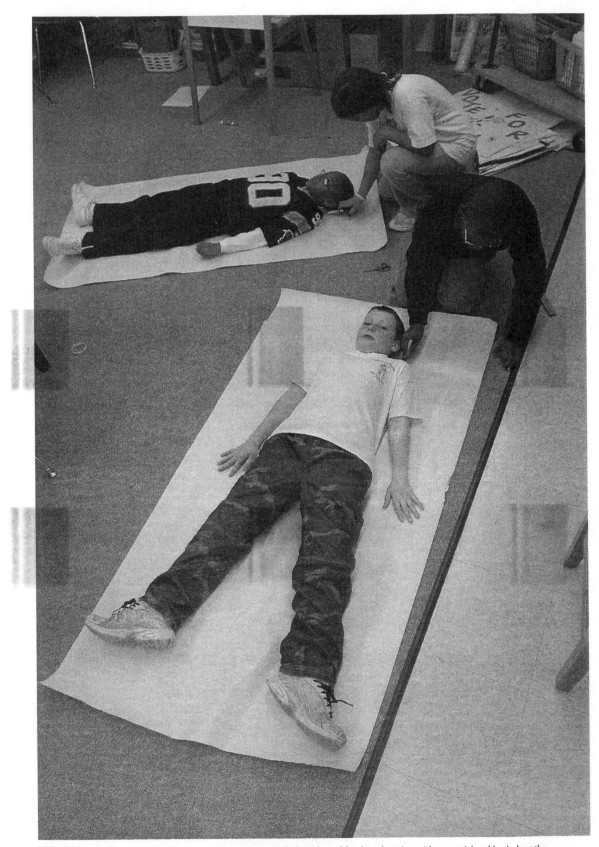

Tracing the outlines of our bodies so we can compare body length and leg length ratios with our crickets' body lengths and leg lengths

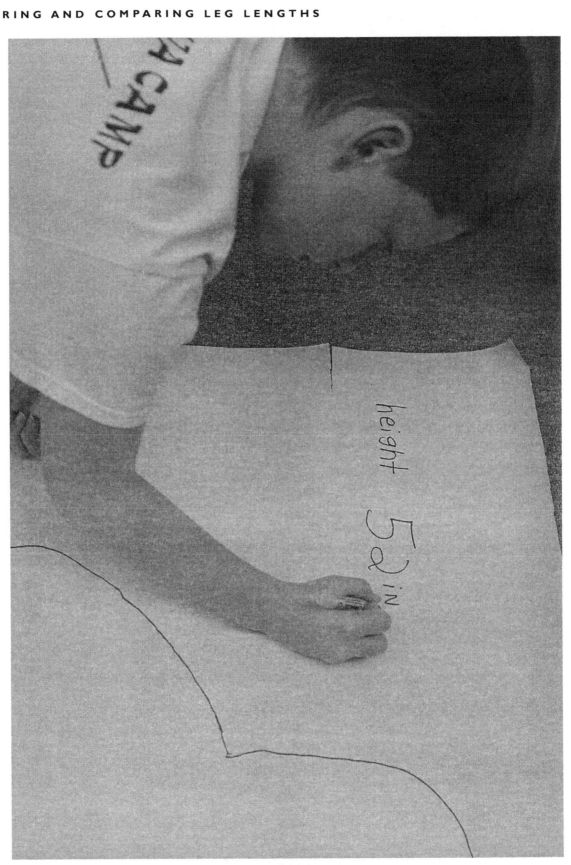

Justin's height

Measuring the length of a cricket

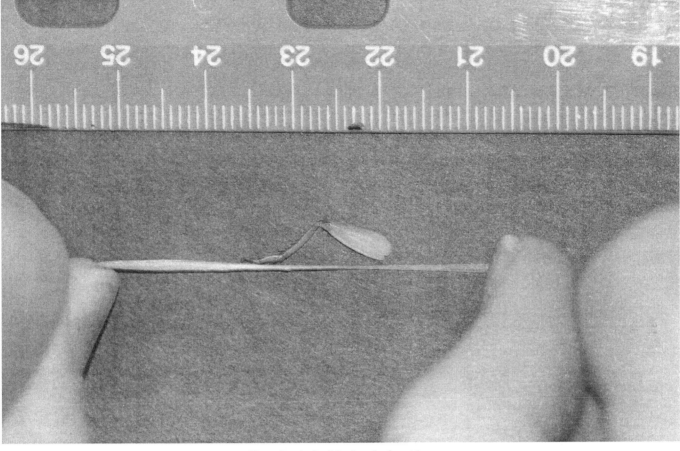

Measuring the back leg length of a cricket

18

JUMPING CRICKETS

ESSENTIAL QUESTIONS

How does cricket jumping ability compare to human jumping ability?
What special body features allow crickets to be such good jumpers?

WHAT DO I NEED?

- One cricket per group
- Two yardsticks per group (one marked and one unmarked)
- One piece of chalk per group
- Pencil
- One measuring tape per group

WHAT DO I DO?

First, answer these two questions.

1. Who will jump farther, a cricket or a human? Why?

2. Will they jump a little farther, or a lot farther? Why?

Then, go outside with your materials.

1. Using the yardstick, measure how far you can jump in the standing broad jump.
2. Do this two times and write your answer in the table below. Using the same yardstick, measure how far a cricket can jump. Do this two times and write your answers in the table below.

Table 18.1.   Comparing My Jumping Ability to a Cricket's Jumping Ability

	Name	Length of First Jump	Length of Second Jump
Student 1			
Student 2			
Student 3			
Student 4			
Cricket			

Who jumped farther, your cricket or you? Why do you think this happened?

_____

_____

_____

_____

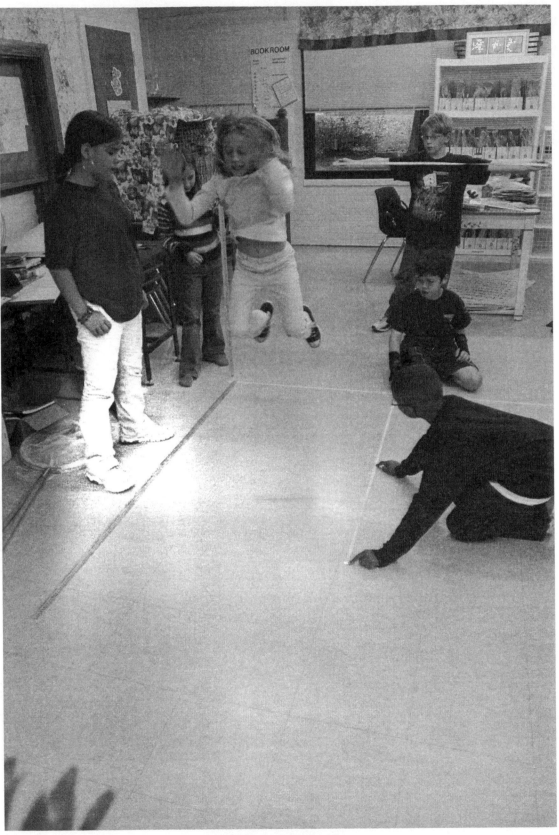

How far can Austin jump?

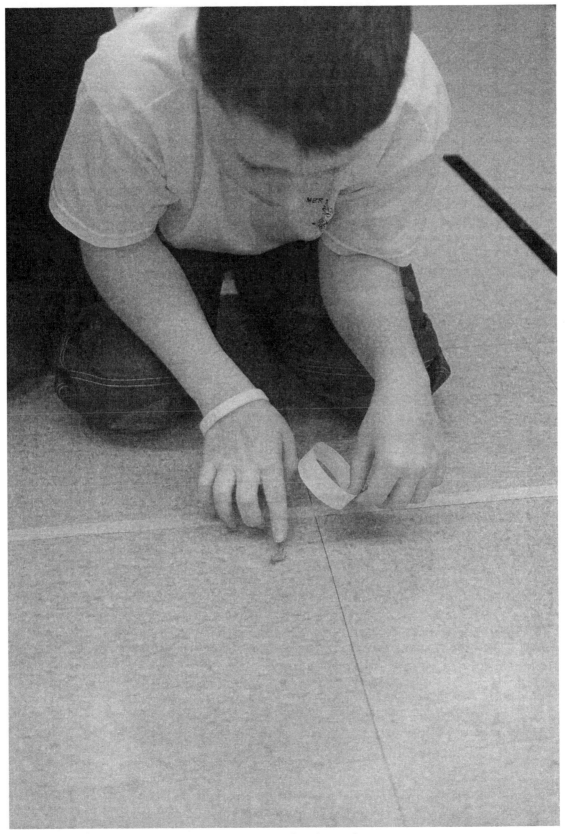

How far can Justin's cricket jump?

SINGING OR CHIRPING, CHIRPING OR SINGING

ESSENTIAL QUESTION

How do crickets chirp or sing?

WHAT DO I NEED?

- Comb
- Fingernail file
- Piece of cardboard

WHAT DO I DO?

Crickets are called *singing insects*. The sounds they make are also called *chirps*. Watch carefully to see if you can tell how male crickets chirp.

Run your fingernail down a comb to make a noise, song, or chirp. How would you describe this sound? Next, move your fingernail file quickly back and forth across a piece of cardboard. Both movements cause the comb or cardboard to vibrate. All sounds are made by vibrating objects. Watch the comb teeth and cardboard and repeat the noise.

Male crickets chirp by moving their wings together quickly. One wing has a hard-ridged vein called a *file*. The other wing has a hard ridge called a *scraper*. When you get home or go outside for recess, you can try to make a loud whistle by blowing on a piece of grass. Pick one blade of grass. Be sure it is straight. Place the blade of grass between your two thumbs. Your thumbs should be oriented with your thumbnails facing you. The blade of grass should be vertical. Now, gently bring your hands up to your mouth and blow through the space in between your thumbs. Look at the photograph at the end of this activity if you need to see a picture of what your hands should look like. When you blow, your breath makes the grass vibrate, which makes a loud noise.

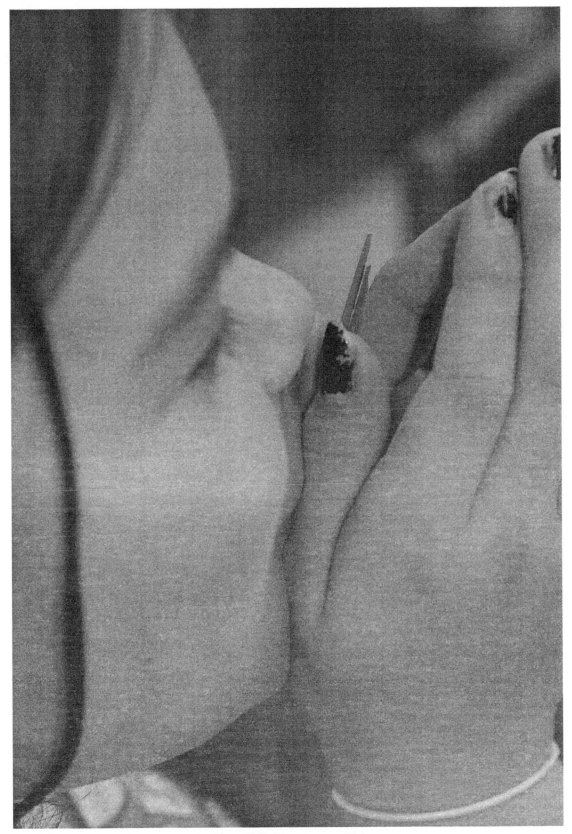

Montana blowing on a grass whistle

20

CHIRPING CRICKETS

ESSENTIAL QUESTION

Which environmental conditions cause crickets to chirp the most?

WHAT DO I NEED?

- Habitat with crickets
- Pencil
- Watch or clock
- Station (will be assigned by teacher)

WHAT DO I DO?

1. Place your cricket habitat at the station that your teacher has assigned to your group. Be very quiet.
2. When your crickets start to chirp, the timekeeper needs to start the stopwatch or look at a clock that has a second hand and say, "go."
3. The timekeeper needs to watch the clock carefully until one minute is up and then call, "stop."
4. Everyone else needs to count how many chirps you hear in one minute.
   a. Record the number of chirps (data) here: _____

Repeat this activity two more times.
   b. Record the number of chirps (data) here: _____
   c. Record the number of chirps (data) here: _____

Add the total number of chirps: _____
Write this number in the table on the next page. Why do you think you needed to count the chirps for three minutes instead of just one minute?

Table 20.1.   When Do Crickets Chirp Most?

Station Description	Temperature (°F/°C)	Total # of Chirps
Bright, warm environment (Windowsill with heating pad)		
Bright, room temperature environment (Windowsill without heating pad)		
Dark, warm environment (Closet with heating pad)		
Dark, room temperature environment (Closet without heating pad)		

READING ABOUT CHIRPING CRICKETS: FACT AND FICTION

ESSENTIAL QUESTION

How can asking questions about crickets help me understand a story about crickets?

WHAT DO I NEED?

- Pencil

WHAT DO I DO?

Turn to the diagram on the next page.

1. In the outer circle of Facts about Crickets, write facts about crickets that you have learned.
2. In the outer circle of Fiction about Crickets, write make-believe information about crickets that you know.

Now, listen to your teacher read a story about crickets.

3. In the inner circle of Facts about Crickets, write facts about crickets that you did not know that were in the story.
4. In the inner circle of Fiction about Crickets, write make-believe information about crickets that you heard in the story.

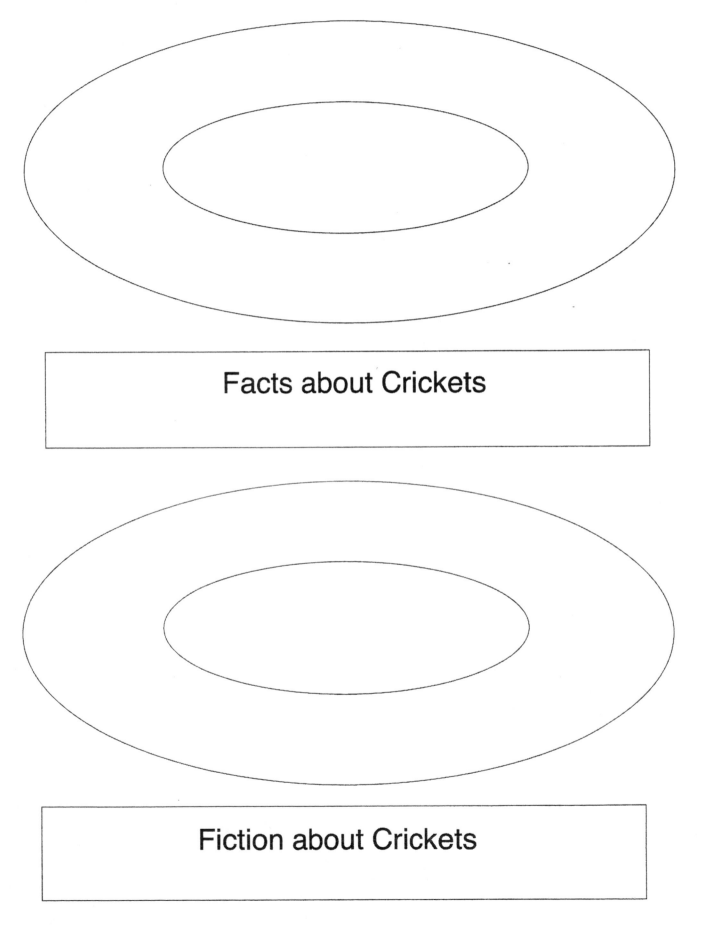

Facts about Crickets

Fiction about Crickets

READERS' THEATER: CRICKETS ON CALL

ESSENTIAL QUESTION

How does writing a Readers' Theatre script about crickets help me remember what I have learned about crickets?

WHAT DO I NEED?

- Pencil

WHAT DO I DO?

After your teacher gives directions, write a Readers' Theatre script about crickets. Remember to use what you have learned about crickets so far to help you, and also make sure that everyone in your group has a part in the play.

㉓

CRICKET LIFE CYCLES

ESSENTIAL QUESTIONS

What stages of life does a cricket go through?
How long do crickets live in each stage?
How is each stage different?

WHAT DO I NEED?

- Crickets in habitat
- Pencil
- Insect boxes

WHAT DO I DO?

Look at the pictures below. Cut them out. Paste them in order in the boxes on the next page.
These pictures show you the three stages of a cricket's life.

Egg	Nymph	Adult

Think about the following questions as you look at each stage of the cricket's life.

1. What does the cricket in the picture look like?

2. How many crickets in this life-cycle stage are in your habitat? _____

3. How long do you think crickets in this life stage will live? _____

4. In the wild, do you think that there are more crickets in the egg, nymph. or adult stage? Why?

MOLTING NYMPHS/AGING CRICKETS

ESSENTIAL QUESTION

What is molting, and why do some animals molt?

WHAT DO I NEED?

- Ruler
- String
- Tweezers or forceps
- Reference materials & Internet access

WHAT DO I DO?

Gently measure the length of 8 crickets in your container. Remember, do not include the ovipositor (the egg-laying body part in females) in the length. Write the lengths in the table below.

Table 24.1. Measuring the Length of Crickets

Cricket	Length of Cricket
1.	
2.	
3.	
4.	
5.	
6.	
7.	
8.	

Why do you think crickets are different lengths?

Why are the students in your class different heights?

Why is your teacher taller than many of the students?

Do you think your crickets are all the same age?

How old is the oldest person you know? _____

How old do you think the oldest cricket is? _____

Who lives longer, humans or crickets? _____

CRICKET MOLTING

Crickets vary in size just like people do in height. Young people grow taller as they age, and crickets grow longer. Crickets shed their skins so that they can grow longer. Many animals shed their skins, their antlers, their hair, their feathers, their horns, or their fur. We lose our complete set of baby teeth as we grow older, and our skin is always shedding, but not all at once. Crickets do shed their exoskeletons all at once as they grow from young nymphs to older adult crickets. You might see some of your crickets molting.

Choose an animal that molts and find information about that animal to answer the following questions:

Name of Animal: _____

Body covering or body parts that are shed:

How often the animal sheds: _____

How and why the animal might be in danger while it is shedding:

CRICKETS IN OUR COUNTRY

ESSENTIAL QUESTION

Where do crickets live and what kinds of crickets live in the USA?

WHAT DO I NEED?

- *Learning Log*

WHAT DO I DO?

On the following pages you will find six maps of the United States. Each map shows where a certain kind of cricket lives. These maps are called *distribution maps*. Only six maps for six different crickets are in your *Learning Log*, but there are lots of other kinds of crickets, thousands (of kinds) of species of crickets. Color the state where you live on each map yellow. Make a list below of the crickets on these maps that live in your state using their common English names.

These crickets live in my state of _____

    1. _____

    2. _____

    3. _____

    4. _____

    5. _____

    6. _____

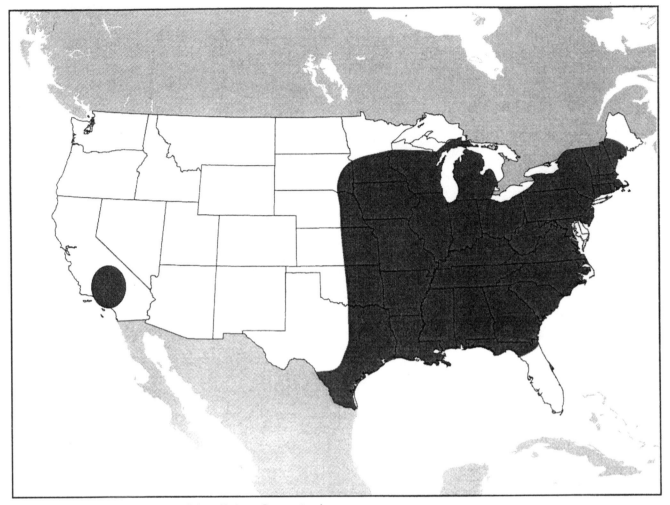

Distribution map of the house cricket *(Acheta Domesticus)*

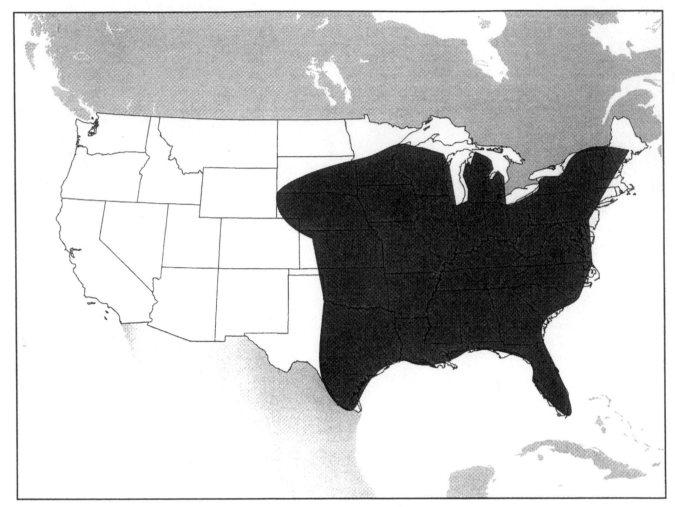

Distribution map of the northern mole cricket *(Neocurtilla Hexadactyla)*

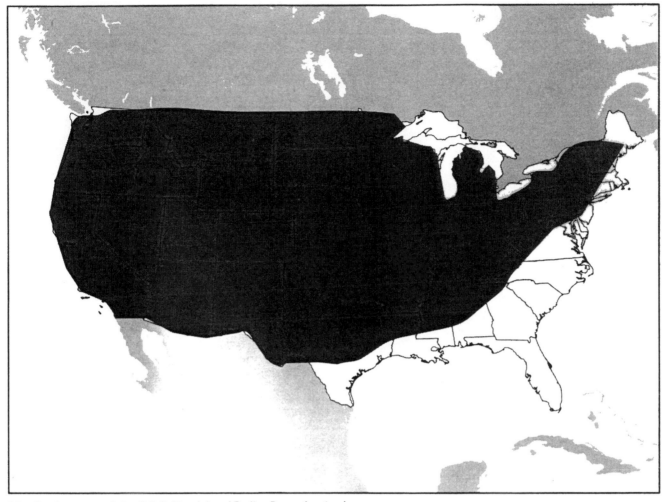

Distribution map of the fall field cricket *(Gryllus Pennsylvanicus)*

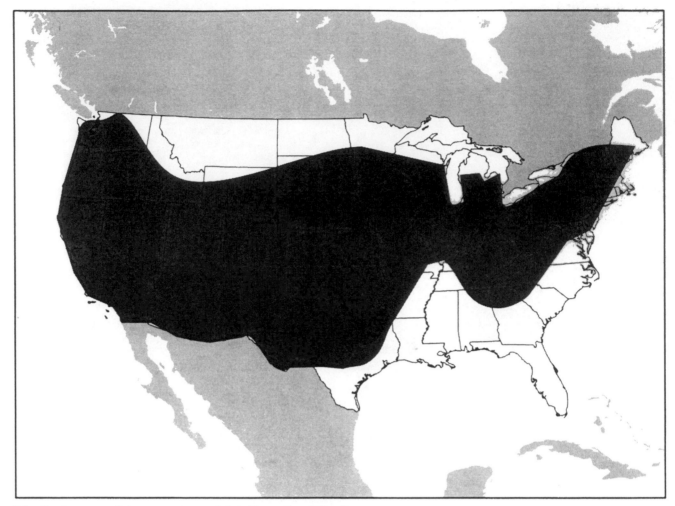

Distribution map of the snowy tree cricket (*Oecanthus Fultoni*)

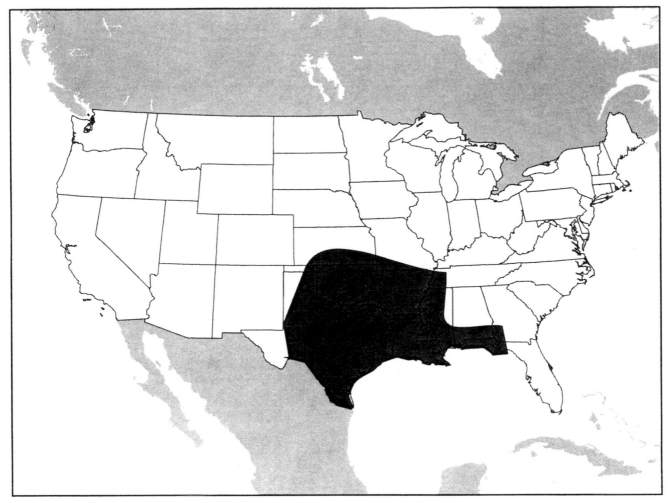

Distribution map of the southwestern field cricket *(Gryllus texensis)*

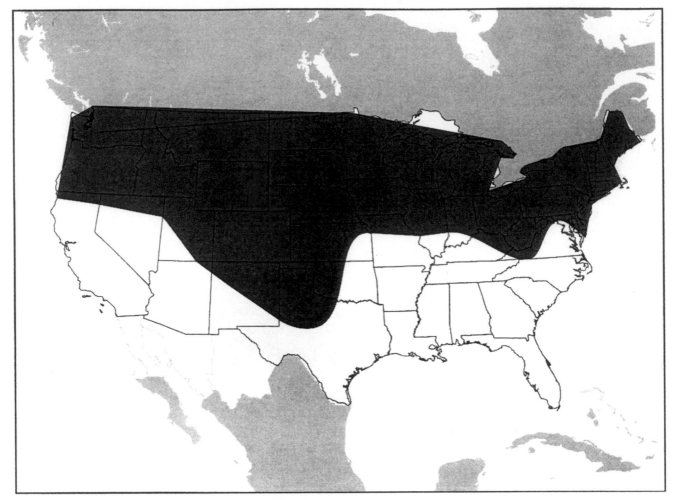

Distribution map of the striped ground cricket (Allonemobius Fasciatus)

Using your maps answer these two questions.

1. Which cricket lives in the most widespread area? _____

2. Which cricket has the most limited range? _____

Why do you think different crickets are found in different places?

_____

_____

_____

_____

26

CRICKETS AROUND THE WORLD

ESSENTIAL QUESTIONS

With respect to worldwide distribution, where do crickets live and what are crickets called in other languages?

Do different cultures view crickets in different ways?

WHAT DO I NEED?

- World Map
- The word "cricket" in other languages

WHAT DO I DO?

Crickets live all over the world. There are house crickets and field crickets, mole crickets, and camel crickets. Cut out the word for cricket in the languages below. Paste these words on the world map or globe where appropriate. Your teacher will help you find countries where the people speak these languages.

cricket	English	grillo	Italian
grillo	Spanish	kricket	German
cricket	French	rilo	Portugese

Studying crickets around the world and figuring out where certain languages are spoken

27

NAMING CRICKETS

ESSENTIAL QUESTIONS

How do scientists name crickets?
How do scientific names differ from common names?
How do names for crickets vary around the world?
Do scientific names vary?

WHAT DO I NEED?

- *Learning Log*
- Pencil

WHAT DO I DO?

There are many types of crickets, but all crickets are animals. You and your classmates are animals, too. So is your teacher. Scientists call all living things by a two-part Latin name. Turn back to your cricket distribution maps. The words in English are the two-part common names for crickets. These English names mean the same thing as the scientific names in Latin. Choose one of the six crickets from your distribution maps found in your state and write its English name and its Latin name below.

Cricket Name (English)
Cricket Name (Latin)

Now, write

1. Your Name (full name)
2. Your Name (nickname)
3. Your Scientific Name (Latin)
[Hint: All people have the very same Latin name.]

Do you have any of the same names as one of your parents, grandparents, brothers, or sisters? If so, which one?

My Name   **Relatives' and Friends' Names that are the same**

For example:

Elizabeth   *Mom and Daughter (all middle names)*

List the name of one or more of your relatives who has one of the same names that you have:

What is the origin of your name? Is it English, Irish, Spanish, African, or do you know?

Me, Montana, and my house cricket, Acheta domesticus

CRICKET CONFERENCE: A HUMANITIES SYMPOSIUM

ESSENTIAL QUESTION

What is the most important information that I have learned about crickets?

WHAT DO I NEED?

- Pencil
- Crayons

WHAT DO I DO?

You will write your own poem about crickets in the same style that Brown uses in *The Important Book*. Use what you have learned about crickets to help you. Draw a picture of a cricket when you have finished.

Crickets

by

The most important thing about crickets is that they _____

Crickets _____

Crickets _____

Crickets _____

But the most important thing about crickets is that they _____

Justin and Glen reading Joyful Noise: Poems for Two Voices

29

CRICKET CONFERENCE: A SCIENTIFIC SYMPOSIUM

 **ESSENTIAL QUESTIONS**

What else can I find out about crickets that I don't know?

How can I discover this information?

How can I best share this information with my classmates?

How can I design and conduct an investigation about crickets?

 **WHAT DO I NEED?**

- Books
- Internet access with a printer
- All equipment and containers used before in *The Cricket Chronicles*

WHAT DO I DO?

Plan a cricket investigation that is different from the other investigations that you have done. Use the plan on the next page. Let your teacher see your plan. Then, conduct your study. Write your final paper. Use the plan included. Be ready to share what you found at the Cricket Conference. Your teacher will tell you how much time you will have for your presentation.

MY CRICKET INVESTIGATION PROPOSAL

What we are trying to find out:

_____

_____

_____

What we will do to answer our question:

_____

_____

_____

What we will observe:

_____

_____

_____

What we think our observations might tell us:

_____

_____

_____

Summary:

_____

_____

_____

MY FINAL CRICKET INVESTIGATION REPORT

What we were trying to find out:

_____

_____

_____

What we did to answer our question:

_____

_____

_____

What our observations were:

_____

_____

_____

What our observations tell us:

_____

_____

_____

Summary:

_____

_____

_____

THE SINGING INSECTS

ESSENTIAL QUESTIONS

Who are the singing insects?
How are singing insects alike and how are they different?

WHAT DO I NEED?

• Singing insects or pictures of singing insects
  (crickets, cicadas, grasshoppers, and katydids)

WHAT DO I DO?

All singing insects are known for their loud songs and long, high jumps. Look at another singing insect and compare it to your cricket. Use the Venn diagram on the next page. Write at least three unique things about crickets (in the left circle), three unique things about your other singing insect (in the right circle), and in the middle write at least three things that both your cricket and the other singing insect have in common. Hint: Think about the insect's leg length, color, length, length of antennae, and location of eyes and ears.

Cricket   Cicada, Grasshopper or Katydid

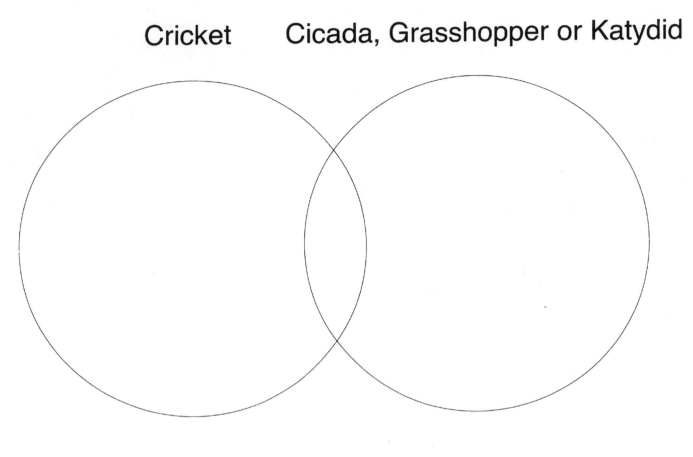

SONGS OF THE SINGERS

ESSENTIAL QUESTION

Can you tell crickets from katydids using only their calls?

WHAT DO I NEED?

- Crickets and katydids or pictures of crickets and katydids

WHAT DO I DO?

Listen carefully as your teacher plays two songs. One song is a cricket chirp, and the other song is a katydid call. Your teacher will play each song several times. Compare the songs. Then match the descriptions of the songs to the insects below.

Cricket chirps = low-frequency, pleasant sounding

Katydid calls = high-frequency, raspy sounding

Call #1 = _____

Call #2 = _____

STUDENT QUESTIONNAIRE

Now that you have completed *The Cricket Chronicles*, please fill out one last questionnaire. What do you know about crickets now? Think about what you learned about crickets in *The Cricket Chronicles*. Write about what you think you learned from this project. Answer the three questions below.

  1. What do crickets look like?

2. What do crickets sound like?

3. Where do crickets live?

In the space below, write one other thing you learned about crickets, and draw a picture of a cricket.

GOODBYE TO *THE CRICKET CHRONICLES*

Dear Student,

I hope that you enjoyed your studies in *The Cricket Chronicles*. Please take this *Learning Log* home to share with your family and friends. Remember to use what you learned about crickets when you read, write, and do other scientific investigations. Remember to use the comprehension strategies that good readers use whenever you read.

Congratulations! You are now an expert on crickets!

Love,
The Cricket Chronicler

Certificate of Completion

This is to certify that _____ has successfully completed

The Cricket Chronicles and now understands more about crickets

than most people do. From now and forever more shall be

_____ known as an amateur grigologist.

_____
Signature of the teacher

_____
Date Completed